Your Muscles
on the Move

By Carole H. Gerber

Wright Group

Photograph and Illustration Credits
Front cover, title page and table of contents: ©Chip Simons/Getty Images; back cover: ©Stock Image/Super Stock; all pages (folio icon): ©PhotoDisc, Inc.; 4-5 (background spread): ©Don W. Fawcett/Photo Researchers, Inc.; 4 (top right): ©Marc Romanelli/Getty Images; 5 (all illustrations): Brian Evans; 6 (top left): ©Corbis, (top to bottom): ©Jim Cummins/Corbis; 7 (bottom center): ©Eric Grave/Phototake, Inc.; 8: ©Mark Maio/Phototake, Inc.; 9 (2 illustrations): Brian Evans; 10 (top left): ©Corbis, (top right): ©Tim Pannell/Corbis; 11 (top right photo): ©Custom Medical Stock Photo, (top right illustration): Brian Evans; 13 (both illustrations): Brian Evans; 14 (bottom left illustration): Brian Evans; 15 (2 illustrations): Brian Evans; 16 (top left): ©Corbis, (top right): ©Nathan Bilow/Getty Images; 17: ©Stock Image/Super Stock, Inc.; 19: ©William H. Edwards/Getty Images; 20 (top right): ©AFP/Corbis; 21 (left to right): ©Bryan-College Station Eagle, Butch Ireland/AP Wide World Photos, (center right): ©Bettmann/Corbis; 22 (background): ©Don W. Fawcett/Photo Researchers, Inc., (top right): ©Myrleen Ferguson Cate/PhotoEdit, Inc., (bottom): ©David Young-Wolff/PhotoEdit, Inc.

Your Muscles: On the Move
Copyright © 2005 Wright Group/McGraw-Hill
Text by Carole H. Gerber

Explore More™ is a trademark of the McGraw-Hill Companies, Inc.

Wright Group/McGraw-Hill
1 Prudential Plaza
130 E. Randolph
Suite 400 Chicago, IL 60601
www.WrightGroup.com

Printed in the United States

ISBN: 1-4045-2833-4
ISBN: 1-4045-2881-4 (6-pack)

2 3 4 5 6 7 8 9 PBM 10 09 08 07 06 05

Contents

Introduction

If your skin were invisible, the first thing you would see would be your muscles. Your muscles cover your bones, give you power, and enable you to move. They work when you want them to, so that you can run, dance, ride a bicycle, or throw a ball. These movements and all others you make are the work of certain kinds of muscles.

There are also muscles deep inside your body that work even without you knowing about them. For example, the muscle tissue that makes up the heart beats on its own. Other muscles help you to breathe, and still others help your body to **digest** food. These muscles do their jobs minute after minute, day after day, and year after year.

Muscles make forty percent of your body's weight—so if you weigh eighty pounds, your muscles weigh about thirty-two pounds. Your body has about 650 muscles, and they work with one another and with other systems in the body so that you can do everything you need to do to stay alive and active.

What kinds of muscles do you have? How do they work? How can you keep them healthy? This book answers these questions, and the answers reveal how your muscles help make you who you are.

The cardiac muscle of the heart constantly contracts and relaxes as it pumps blood.

Smooth muscles in blood vessels contract slowly and gently to move blood through the body.

The skeletal muscles in the legs power your lower body. They enable you to walk, run, and jump.

1

The Three Types of Muscles

There are three types of muscles—skeletal muscles, smooth muscles, and cardiac muscle. Each type has a certain appearance. Skeletal muscles are made of long thin bundles of muscle fibers. Smooth muscle fibers are arranged in layers that crisscross each other. Cardiac muscle looks like—but works very differently than—skeletal muscle.

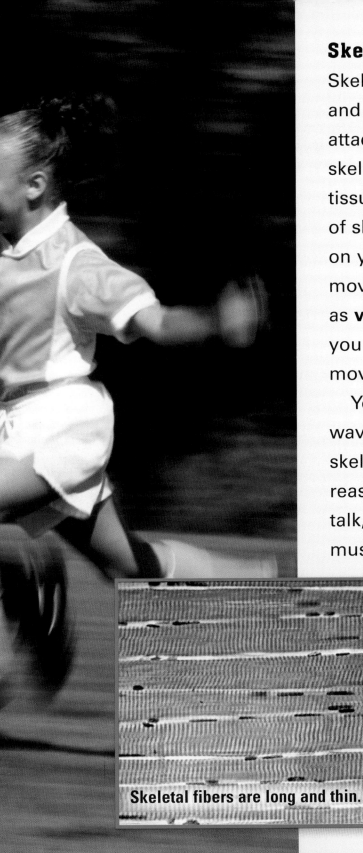

Skeletal Muscles

Skeletal muscles, the largest and strongest muscles, are attached to the bones of the skeleton by tough, cordlike tissues called tendons. The job of skeletal muscles is to pull on your bones so that you can move. These muscles are known as **voluntary** muscles, because you decide when and how to move them.

You are able to jump and wave your arms because of skeletal muscles. They are the reason you can clap your hands, talk, and nod your head. These muscles enable you to grip a pencil and type on a keyboard. Can you think of other actions your skeletal muscles enable you to do?

Skeletal fibers are long and thin.

Smooth Muscles

Smooth muscles control the body's **involuntary** movements, which happen without your control. They are shorter than skeletal muscles, and they also **contract** more slowly. They line the walls of many body organs, including the stomach, the intestines, the bladder, and the **uterus** (YOO tuhr uhs). They line the insides of **blood vessels,** too. The job of many smooth muscles is to push fluids and other substances through the hollow parts of the body by gently contracting and relaxing. Other smooth muscles cause round openings in the body, such as the pupils of the eyes, to grow larger or smaller.

Smooth muscles surround the pupils, the round, dark openings of the eyes. These muscles relax to open the pupils and let in more light. They contract to make the pupils smaller.

Muscle Extremes		
Extreme	**Name**	**Location**
Fastest muscle	orbicularis oculi	around eyelids
Smallest muscle	stapedius	inside ear
Widest muscle	latissimus dorsi	middle back
Largest muscle	gluteus maximus	buttocks

Cardiac Muscle

The heart is the only place in the body where **cardiac** muscle is found. This type of involuntary muscle is the powerhouse of the body. Certain cells in cardiac muscle tissue cause the heart to beat automatically 100,000 times a day. This is truly strong, tough, hardworking muscle tissue!

As it beats, the heart pumps blood throughout the body, delivering **oxygen** and nutrients to the body's cells and carrying away **carbon dioxide** and other wastes. The heart beats slowly when you are at rest. When you exercise, it automatically speeds up to send more blood and oxygen to the body's muscles.

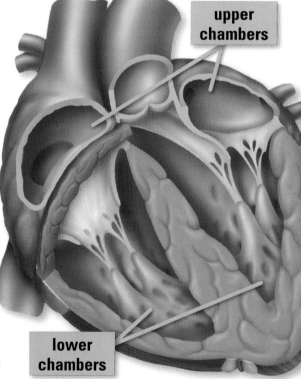

upper chambers

lower chambers

The muscles of the heart contract when it beats. This forces blood from the upper chambers into the lower chambers and out through the major blood vessels.

2

How Do Muscles Work?

Have you ever flexed your arm to make a muscle? When you do this, the top of your arm bulges out and gets firmer as the skeletal muscle fibers contract. The fibers grow shorter and thicker as they pull on the arm bone. The energy that muscles need to work comes from food. Your body first changes the food into fat or **glucose,** a type of sugar. Your body then uses the fat and glucose as fuel to power the muscle system.

Pushing and Pulling

Skeletal muscles can only pull on bones. They cannot push bones. That is why skeletal muscles work in pairs. One muscle, or set of muscles, pulls a bone one way. Then another muscle or set pulls it back the other way. While one muscle in the pair contracts, the other muscle relaxes and lengthens.

The biceps muscle and the triceps muscle are one such pair. The biceps muscle, the one that bulges when you flex your arm to make a muscle, contracts to raise the forearm, while the triceps muscle, which is on the back of the upper arm, contracts to lower the forearm. Can you think of other places in the body where pairs of muscles work together in a similar way?

biceps

triceps

The biceps and triceps muscles work together to move your arms.

11

Nerve Signals

What causes muscles to contract in the first place? The brain sends messages to the muscles in the form of electrical signals that travel through **nerve cells.** These signals trigger the muscles to contract. Voluntary muscles and involuntary muscles are controlled by different parts of the brain.

The part of the brain called the cerebellum (sair uh BEHL uhm) is in charge of voluntary muscles. The signals sent by the cerebellum travel through nerve cells called **motor neurons,** which run down the spine. From there, motor neurons branch out into every part of the body, each one connecting to a muscle fiber.

Nerve signals make muscles move by causing chemical changes in the muscles. When the brain sends a message to bend the left arm, the signal travels through nerve cells to the fibers of the biceps muscle. In these fibers, a chemical change occurs.

In Their Own Words

"A lot of people don't know that [the triceps muscle makes up the bulk of the arm]. They just look at big arms and think it's all biceps. The triceps are extremely important. You have to work on both."

—MICHAEL PITTMAN, RUNNING BACK WITH THE TAMPA BAY BUCCANEERS

This chemical change causes the biceps to contract, and the arm bends. This entire process happens in just a fraction of a second!

Smiles, frowns, and all the other expressions on a person's face are caused by voluntary muscles, too. The muscles of the face attach to each other or to the skin. The contraction of just a few muscles can change the expressions on a face to display all of an individual's moods and feelings. It takes forty-three muscles to frown but only fourteen to smile!

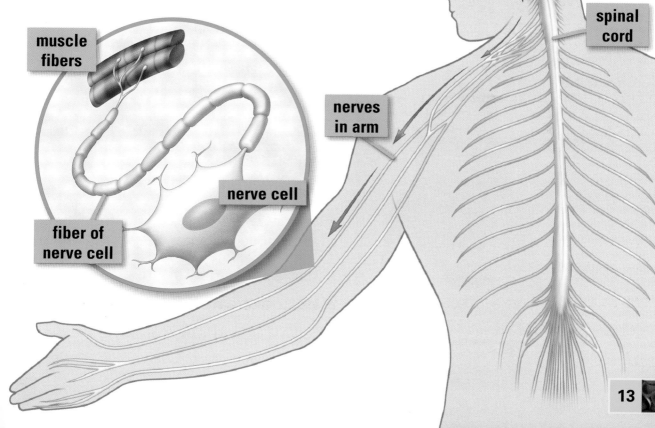

Nerve cells deliver electrical messages from the cerebellum that cause muscle fibers to contract.

cerebellum

spinal cord

muscle fibers

nerves in arm

nerve cell

fiber of nerve cell

The body's smooth muscles are controlled by nerve signals from the brain stem, the part of the brain that connects to the spinal cord. Smooth muscles are always busy pushing something. They push food through the digestive system, urine out of the bladder, blood through the blood vessels, and waste out of the intestines. When it is time for a baby to be born, smooth muscles even push the child out into the world!

When smooth muscles are working correctly, a person is not usually aware of them. However, when problems develop in smooth muscles, such as in the stomach, they are suddenly very noticeable. Pain is usually the first clue that something is wrong with smooth muscles.

Cardiac muscle works differently from skeletal muscles and smooth muscles. Cardiac muscle has special tissue that gives the heart a built-in system of contracting and relaxing.

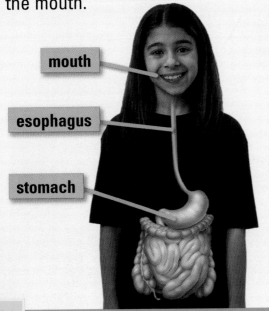

mouth

esophagus

stomach

14

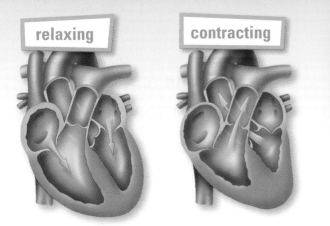

relaxing   contracting

Blood flows in when the heart relaxes and flows out when the heart contracts.

The special tissue sends out electrical signals that cause different parts of the heart to contract at the right time.

Chemical changes in the body can sometimes affect the heart's rhythm, or beat. Such changes may be caused by fear, excitement, or other strong emotions. Nerve signals sent from the brain stem can change the speed at which the heart beats. Can you remember the last time you noticed an increase or decrease in the rhythm of your heart?

Your Changing Pulse

Measure your pulse, or heart rate, before and after you exercise. Notice the change in the rate at which the heart beats. Here's how to do it:

1. Place the first two fingertips of your right hand on the large blood vessels on the underside of your left wrist. You will feel your pulse as your heart contracts and pushes blood through the vessels.

2. Count the number of beats for 15 seconds. Multiply by 4 to get the number of beats per minute. (Example: If you count 18 heartbeats in 15 seconds, your pulse is 18 x 4 = 72.) Most people have pulses between 60 and 85.

Always stretch your muscles before you exercise.

Keeping Muscles Healthy

Muscles are meant to move. If muscles are not used regularly, they will grow weak. Regular exercise will keep your skeletal muscles and heart healthy and strong—and exercise can be fun! Riding a bike, jumping on a trampoline, dancing, and climbing a tree are all good activities for muscles. Good exercise habits begun in childhood may stay with you the rest of your life.

Protect Your Muscles

Athletes warm up their muscles by stretching them before they use them. Stretching muscles makes them more flexible and causes more blood to flow into them. Flexible muscles contract and relax easily and are less likely to be strained, or torn. Before exercising, you should also drink plenty of water. If your body does not have enough water, certain chemicals in your muscles can get out of balance during vigorous exercise. This can lead to muscle cramps, very painful contractions of muscles that last a long time.

Muscle cramps can also happen after exercise. So to end an intense workout, many athletes gradually slow down the pace of exercise rather than come to a sudden stop. This helps the heart and muscles readjust to a normal level of activity.

Did You Know?

Running, biking, and swimming are types of aerobic exercises. Such exercises promote health by producing a rapid heart rate for long periods, allowing large amounts of oxygen to go to the muscles. The increased oxygen supply helps the body produce more energy and work more efficiently (less wastefully).

Another way to keep muscles healthy is to treat them with care. When you bend to pick up something heavy, it is a good idea to bend at the knees instead of the back. This will keep the strain off the muscles in your back. Carrying a heavy, overstuffed backpack can also hurt your back muscles. You can keep your back healthy by carrying only those books that you'll need right away.

Good posture when sitting at a computer can prevent muscle strain in the neck, back, and legs. Your head should be balanced over your spine, and your feet should stay flat on the floor.

Some computers and keyboards are designed to prevent muscle strain. Designers who specialize in ergonomics create products so that people can use them in safe, healthy ways.

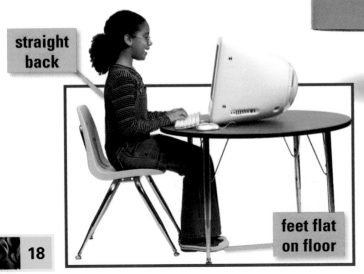

bent knees

straight back

feet flat on floor

These pictures show the proper ways to pick up a heavy object and sit at the computer.

Muscles need protein, which are in such foods as meat and eggs, and carbohydrates, which are in fruit, bread, and pasta.

Muscles Need the Right Food

The food you eat determines how your body performs and what it looks like. Protein helps to build, maintain, and repair muscles. A diet that does not include enough protein can result in serious health problems. Muscles may waste away, making a person feel weak and tired. The body may not grow well, and a person may get diseases more easily.

Many foods, including eggs, meat, fish, milk, grains, beans, and nuts, are excellent sources of protein. However, people need more than protein for their muscles. It is also important to eat foods containing carbohydrates (car boh HY drayts), such as fruit, bread, and pasta. These foods provide glucose, which fuels muscles. Another important substance for your muscles is potassium, which helps control muscle activity. Sources of potassium include leafy green vegetables, bananas, and many other foods.

Spotlight:
When Muscles Do Not Work Right

Muscle conditioning helps prevent cramps.

A number of health problems affect muscles. These problems range from minor irritations to life-threatening disorders.

Muscles become strained when the fibers in them overstretch and get torn. Muscles may have long cramps or shorter spasms for many reasons. These painful contractions can be caused by exercising too hard or by accidents, such as falls. Have you ever gotten a cramp in your leg while you were sleeping? Such cramps are very common, though scientists are not sure why they happen. Cramps are most common in the calf or lower back.

Serious muscle disorders are not as easily treated as strains and cramps. Muscular dystrophy (DIHS truh fee) affects the skeletal muscles by causing them to waste away. There are several forms of muscular dystrophy, all of which are inherited at birth.

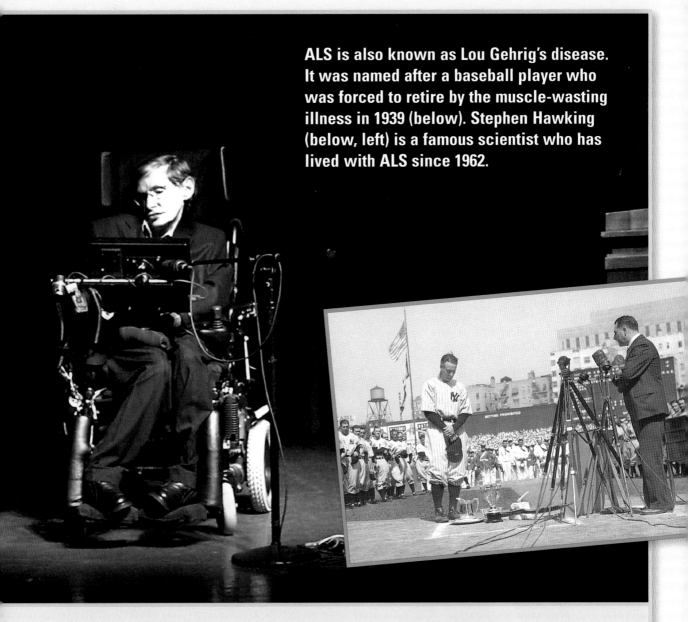

ALS is also known as Lou Gehrig's disease. It was named after a baseball player who was forced to retire by the muscle-wasting illness in 1939 (below). Stephen Hawking (below, left) is a famous scientist who has lived with ALS since 1962.

Amyotrophic lateral sclerosis (ay mee uh TROH fik LAT uhr uhl skluh ROH sihs), or ALS for short, affects the nerve cells that tell muscles what to do. It causes the nerve cells in the spine and brain to break down, blocking messages from the brain to the muscles.

Conclusion

All the different muscles in your body have special jobs to do. Your skeletal muscles power your movements, your smooth muscles power your organs and blood vessels, and your cardiac muscle powers your heart.

Exercising keeps your muscles strong, and stretching keeps them flexible. Eating a variety of healthy foods gives them the fuel they need to perform. Maintaining good posture and using your muscles wisely helps to protect them.

Exercising and eating well helps people develop healthy muscles.

In return for taking good care of your muscles, they will work every minute of every day to keep you alive and in motion.

Glossary

blood vessels hollow tubes through which blood flows

carbon dioxide gas produced as waste product by living things as part of a process called respiration

cardiac having to do with the heart

contract to become shorter or tighter

digest to break down food so the body can use it for energy

ergonomics the science of designing products so that people can use them in safe, healthy ways

fibers long, thin cells that make up muscles

glucose sugar that provides energy to muscles and other parts of the body

involuntary working automatically, without a person's control

motor neurons nerve cells that connect to muscle fibers

nerve cells cells that carry electrical signals throughout the body

oxygen gas needed by the cells of the body for life

uterus organ inside a female's body where a baby develops and grows

voluntary describes something that a person can control

23

Index